Mother Lines

poems by

Shawna Ervin

Finishing Line Press
Georgetown, Kentucky

Mother Lines

ACKNOWLEDGEMENTS

Grateful acknowledgement is made to the editors of the following journals
in which these poems first appeared:

Euphony: "Accused"
Evening Street Review: "Birthmom"
Hiram Poetry Review: "Packing List to Meet my Son's Birthmother"
The Door is Ajar: "Letter"
Talking River: "Reflection"
Steam Ticket: "Autism's ABCs," "Checkout Line," "Regurgitated Lies,"
"Soothing"

Publisher: Leah Maines
Editor: Christen Kincaid
Cover Art: Lisa Lord, Lilo Photography; lilophoto.com
Author Photo: SkigenDigital
Cover Design: Elizabeth Maines McCleavy

Printed in the USA on acid-free paper.
Order online: www.finishinglinepress.com
        also available on amazon.com

Author inquiries and mail orders:
Finishing Line Press
P. O. Box 1626
Georgetown, Kentucky 40324
U. S. A.

Table of Contents

Checkout Line

"They are beautiful,"
you say, your cart piled
with a week's worth of what you want. In front

of me, you turn, stare. "Thank you," I mutter, knowing
from your eyes, your stance, that you have more
to say. My son, my daughter,

peer at me from the gum and Legos.
"Can I, can I, can I? Just one? If we share? Please?"
You. With a quick push of your cart,

"How much did they cost? What happened
to their real parents? Are they real
brother and sister? Oh, you know what I mean."

"What do you mean by real?"
I've practiced this answer, the grimace, the shifting
of my hips, pulling my shoulders back. What

do you mean by tossing *real*
at me, my kids, their brown
skin, almond eyes, their childhood

anger growing at the collective
you? You think they didn't hear? I know
what you mean. I know. And you,

what do you know? "Priceless,"
I answer. Tell me again
what you mean by real. What is it you want

to know? Your food is bagged, yet you
linger. "Priceless," I say
again. "Real." You know what I mean.

Packing List to Meet My Son's Birth Mother

Socks and underwear pushed into plastic bags, air squished out—a wrinkly mass of yellow and red and blue, camouflage. An extra pair just in case.

Passports and IDs, a ceramic ornament, photos from the time she missed with him, a calendar from Colorado, ambiguous, impersonal.

Say the first name he had, the name that means jewel. Say, "That is how she knows you." Try to explain what it means, hope I have it right, know I can't.

Tell stories of meeting him, a scared baby, how he still has the same smile. Does it look like hers? Wonder if they will see in each other something that was missing. Will I know what to say, offer the right amount of distance?

Share.

Toothbrushes and shampoo, lotion and Benadryl. Consider using Benadryl for the long flight. Consider not feeling guilty.

Slippers and pajamas. Won. A secret word and backup plan, in case he can't handle the meeting, in case I can't.

Enjoy my son's reaction to looking like everyone. Point out my freckles and hazel eyes, joke. Hope he can too.

Nice pants and sweaters, new socks, to impress what she might remember, encourage what she will forget, enforce my place as a mother, too.

The fancy camera, to see in photos later what I will miss that day, what I cannot imagine before.

Subway map of Seoul, email addresses, schedule of meeting times, contact information for adoption agency.

Don't get lost.

Give and receive gifts with two hands, a bow, a nod, thank you, thank you. Kahm sa hamida. Kahm sa hamida. Expect laughter. Say it anyway.

Questions. To begin conversations. Questions without answers. Should I ask about the father?

Feel. All of it.

Retrieve something tangible, a souvenir, a smell. To know it was real, that it still is. Hold it.

Hope that he understands love, that it's enough for now, that he knows what to take and what to leave for another time.

Long for more time, more words in common, more of each other, more.

Resent loss, this pain, his and mine and hers, and what brought us together. Relish what brought us together.

Promise to return. Hope we mean it, that she does too.

Leave incomplete.

En Español

All of my mom's thinking
was in Spanish, *mira mi bolsa,*

her purse, on the restaurant bathroom floor,
my eye pressed to the snap on the front,

my other eye memorized the tile pattern.
I looked for places

where the grout was chipped
away, applied unevenly. The stall

door opened. *You don't have to watch
it that closely.* Sneering laughter. *Pobrecita.*

Another woman washed her hands, watched
Mamá in the mirror. Soap landed

on the counter, Mamá patted my head, a little
too hard. I would cringe later, alone,

when no one was watching. *Poor
little girl,* Mamá translated. The woman

rinsed, dried, left. Mamá at home:
Siéntate por favor. Es hora de comer.

I sat. Bowed my head. Waited. The eggs
fried the same as every other morning,

a shiny crust at the edges. I pushed it
under the lip of my plate. *Pásame*

la sal y pimiento. I passed the salt and pepper,
placed them before the newspaper held high,

Mamá somewhere behind it. *Can I*
have some juice? Mamá's hands clenched

the sides of the newspaper, shook it, corrected
me. *¿Jugo de naranja? ¿Por qué no leche?*

She sloshed the juice into my glass,
spilled. I cleaned up. *Mantequilla, por favor.*

I gave in, softened. This,
her table. *¿Pan tostado? Si.*

Birthmom

I.
Hello. What else is there to say
to you, who shares his eyes,
round face, brown skin? I don't speak
your language, you mine.

You'd like to meet
him, you wrote. He begged.
I bow, nudge him
forward, to you.

He squeezes my hand. *It's okay,*
I say, *if you want
her to hold you, if you don't, if you need
me to take you away*

from here. I will remember
your orange nail polish, how your hands
fit, his hand yours, your hand his.
Please, stop smiling his smile.

I am brave, not crying, blinking,
my hand not sweating, my voice
not trembling. The blinds are dusty. You pull
him close, he looks to me. I want

to adopt you too. The couch
upholstery is thin.
A stray thread dangles
at the hem of my pants.

He nods fast,
smiles wide.
I pat my lap. "Not yet,"
he says, "not yet."

II.
He screamed the night
after we met you, like we were tearing
his skin off. He refused
to move in the airport security line. "You can't
make me leave. I love her."

Home again, he ran down the street, away
from our white faces. I wrapped
around him tighter than he wanted, hoped
he would think of you. My bruises
are proof love can break

us. He won't hold
my hand because he held yours. He tells me
about his toenails, how they curl like yours; his laugh,
reminds me of you. I kiss
his cheek; the top of his head rests
on my chest. I don't tell him to let go
when he twists my hair around
his finger, when it hurts.

He was carried
into school this morning kicking,
biting. He begged to go home.
He meant here. He meant there.

Gift

Mom, I would have brought you
a pinch pot, a new painting, my best
attempt so far

offered it to you,
please, take this, please look at it, please.
It's just for you.

Orange and blue, your favorite
colors. I would have picked fresh lilacs
on the way home

from school, carried them close,
placed them in your hand, waited, wanted
to hear, "Thank you.

It's beautiful, you made
this all by yourself? I am honored."
You threw the pot away.

The flowers too.
You said that's where they belong. Afraid,
I nod. I nod.

Too many mistakes. Yes,
ugly. Yes, awful. Yes, terrible.
I know. Me too.

Doljabi

(Korean traditional ceremony for a baby's first birthday)

In the photo, son, you are serious,
your lips slightly puckered
over one tooth. Pink
vest, Easter green sleeves, silk
creased at the elbows. Stripes
of brightly colored fabric measure
your smallness, this birthday,
your first. You sit in your grandma's
chair, your legs straight out, the short back
dwarfing you, all we have to learn
about you. The black hat, stamped
with gold characters, sits lopsided
on your bald head, slips over one eye. You
seem comfortable
in the unexplained,
crawl to the table, your future,
look at the brush, money, thread, rice,
choose the hammer. You will be
a craftsman, able to build, fix
what is broken. You put the hammer
in your mouth. We take it
from you, laugh. You cry,
point. It is yours, who
you will be, who you already are.

Bedtime

Mom, do you remember my first
day here, with you, this family? She pulls
my arm close, wraps around it, rests my hand
on her full stomach. She is eight, her hair silky
and black, almost to her waist. She tugs
at her blanket, pale pink, tips her head
sideways, grins, black eyes shrinking
into the darkness of her bedroom. *Please?*
She is stalling. *Just a little?* "Okay,"
I say, "just the beginning. I took you outside."
Her cheeks swell into a smile, the hallway light warm
on her ivory skin. On her bed, I lean against the wall, feel
cold through my hair. Her mouth takes the shape
of my words, the story familiar. "I watered
the pansies. They were pink and purple
that year, a few white. It was hot
for September. You were mesmerized
by the water. You squatted in the dress, stained
with seaweed and formula, that you wore
on the long plane ride from Korea to Denver when
I bounced you in the aisle for hours;
you screamed at me, a stranger. You cupped
your hands, the water filled them, ran over, lifted
your hands to your lips, drank. The water
dripped down the front of your dress.
You were soaked." *Mmmm hmmm.*
Her eyes close. She flops on her back, her mouth
slightly open; her bottom lip forms a point.
Her pajamas twist, her shirt pulls up
to show her belly button. "That's when I knew,"
I whisper, lift my arm from under
her to her hair. My fingers catch on tangles, gently
work them loose, "you had been loved
and would let me love you too."

Fear

What if a burglar comes tonight? What if
there's a tornado, a fire, a flood?
What if you forget me, fall off a cliff?

What if my scab comes off and there's blood?
What if I swallow a spider? What if the toilet clogs?
What if, when you're asleep, I throw up blood?

What if someone kills you, my sister, the dog?
What if a shooter pulls the fire alarm?
What if they fill the school with fog?

What if my sister falls for someone's charm,
if they hurt her, if she doesn't come back?
What if I see them take her, grab her arm?

What if I can't yell, if I can't keep track
of where, when, the gun, the man, the woman?
I dreamed last night that all of us were attacked.

What if the policeman or fireman
falls, gets hurt, can't help me after only one whiff
of smoke, doesn't come? What if I forget the plan?

Accused

Years after she's gone, my body craves my mother's touch.
God works all things together for good.
Betrayal lingers; she chose to leave me.
Everything happens for a reason.

God works all things together for good.
Hunger burned in my stomach; I forgot how to cry.
Everything happens for a reason.
Dad's body heavy on mine, pink nightgown peeled back.

Hunger burned in my stomach; I forgot how to cry.
God will never give you more than you can handle.
Dad's body heavy on mine, pink nightgown peeled back.
God wants you to forgive. He must be trying to teach you something.

God will never give you more than you can handle.
The police report says "Aggravated Incest."
God wants you to forgive. He must be trying to teach you something.
My name in the victim box.

The police report says "Aggravated incest."
Betrayal lingers; she chose to leave me.
My name in the victim box.
Years after she's gone, my body craves a mother's touch.

Soothing

I know you're angry, that you hate me. I know
I'm not your birth mom. I don't look like you.
Please don't throw your pizza, your fork.

Do you want to go into your room, hug your blanket?
I'm not your birth mom. I can't look like you.
I wish I could take you to Seoul, to her. I wish she lived here.

I wish I could be her, be me, be exactly what you need.
I'm not your birth mom. I'm not who you want.
Please don't slam the door. Please don't scream at your sister.

I want to help. I want to comfort you.
I'm not your birth mom. I'm not the mom you need.
Listen to my voice. Hush now, breathe.

Do you want a hug, a popsicle, a song, a book?
I'm not your birth mom. I'm the mom who is here.
I'm here, right here.

Bedtime

Wrap your body around my arm, baby girl, rest your cheek there, let me spread my fingers across your belly, imagine you fit in my hand, that I can stretch large enough to keep you safe. Tell me what you hope to dream tonight, the story already forming in your mind. You can fly, fall into a cloud, and rest there. Hold my arm tight, feel its promise to stay, linger, wish you forever. Will you know this feeling after you have grown, after you have left this house, this room, being tucked in? Will your back remember, your hair, your hand on mine, your feet draped over my legs? Will you always know this, know how to give this to your baby one day, know the safety of bedtime? Your breath slows. I let my hand rest on your back, lean my head against the cold wall, wish I had known this, the feel of a mom's hand on my back, a mom's low voice, a mom. I close my eyes. In the dark I imagine a mom staying until I'm ready for her to go.

Regurgitated Lies

Your birth parents were poor, young, too young. They weren't ready to be parents, didn't want to quit college, weren't ready to get married, lost touch with each other, were scared, so scared. They knew you needed more than they could give, chose this for you, this house, this life, this country, this state. They loved you enough to choose, to know, to see ahead to the glossy future. They loved you when they signed the papers, when they said yes to you going to another country, when they left you at the hospital, returned to the life they'd had before. Don't think about your birth mom leaving alone, how her previous life had ended, how she was no longer the same person, how she grieved that day, still does. We were ready. Prepared, educated, older, wiser. We were waiting for you, only for you, of course for you. It was serendipity, grace, meant to be that you ended up in our family. Don't think about how that implies your loss was also meant to be, that not having your birth parents was designed. You are ours now, just ours, forever. Don't think about how forever isn't real for anyone, no matter how much they love each other. We knew how to love, wanted you, wanted so much. We chose you, you chose us, the agency matched us, we are all lucky, lucky, so lucky to have each other, to have found each other, lucky we lost what we did to all be together. We are here now. They are there. What are they doing? Is your birthday still painful for your birthmom? Will it always be painful for you? Don't think about how I cannot be enough. Think about here, about now, what we share, not how love is not enough, how it's never even close to enough.

Reflection

I listen to the mirror, its truth.
It lies.

That is my mother, not me.
Her eyes laugh in creases, her second toe bends the wrong way,
summer freckles cover her shoulders.

That is her chin, her short arms, her brown eyes, hair that gently waves.
Our craving for cheese, a nasal giggle,
the propensity to say things like propensity.
Her reflection. My image.

My neck is creased like hers; my knuckles puckered.
Her hands that wouldn't hold mine, are now mine.
I reach for us. The mirror is cold.
I cannot forget.

Her sneer catches on my mouth.
The myth of *we* breaks.
I cannot forgive.

Morning

He greets me by the edge
of my bed, the same as yesterday, the days
before. This, our moment in the dark,
his head barely past the mattress. "What are we doing

today? What's for breakfast?" His round
face, the same perfectly round face
I met when he was one, toothless, bald. He has
thick, black hair now, the same piercing

eyes that want answers: *I am*
your mom. I am here.
You are safe. Safe. I will keep
you safe. He reaches for my hand,

swings it around, up, holds
my focus. He's stronger now. *School today.*
It's Tuesday. Do you remember
what special you have? You have speech. You'll see

Ms. Abby, Ms. Michelle. You can
check the lunch menu on the fridge
when you're ready. Today
is the 18th. Do you know

what that looks like? 18?
Do you know what you will be
like at 18, if you'll live
here, with me

or somewhere else? Will you need
me to go over the day?
Will I hope you'll make it
through another day, worry

you'll have a meltdown, hurt
yourself? Will you still
come to me, hold
my hand, ask, assume I know?

"Mom, when will you pick me
up? What will we do after school? What's
for dinner? What will you do
today? Where will you be if I need you?"

Autism's ABCs

Autism says no, don't come close, not like that.
Bring me my blue blanket,
crouch before me, whisper,
don't touch me,
don't talk loudly,
don't make any sudden moves, don't
erase me under this label.
Feel it under your nails like dirt; let it screech on your chalkboard. Do
you hear the way it
grows with me,
grows louder, stronger,
grows around me like a cape
holds me closer than you can, even
if you love me, want to be the one to say, can I
just give you one hug,
just hold your hand,
just sit near you,
just one minute, it's just me, mom. I don't
know how to make it better.
Leave me alone, leave me here, go now, please go,
mom, please I am begging you to go,
now. Now. Now. No. No. Don't
open the door until I ask, until I am ready, until
please, mom, you can't help me, but please don't
quit asking, quit reaching. There is no
revenge, reward, repair in this relentless
scene that replays over and over,
tonight at dinner, yesterday at bedtime, tomorrow after school. Autism's
undercurrent
venerable and
wild, an
explosion, an unmet
yearning, a
zenith of failing to understand.

Bedtime

I already told you to brush your teeth.
No, that noise was only your imagination.
Wait, what is this you say you need?

Overnight, I promise, that bean will not morph into a weed.
Do you believe me? I am tired despite my facial expression.
Now, what do you think you need?

A drink of water, a toy left in my car, you think your toenail bleeds?
The meatloaf from dinner left you with indigestion?
I already told you to brush your teeth.

We can finish this book tomorrow. I know you like to read.
That feeling in your head is only congestion.
Oh my. Again? Yet another need?

I find myself willing to plead
to move beyond this intermission.
Please, please go brush your teeth.
Another hug? Is that what you need?

Tag

"You're it." She runs
around the large honey locust tree, ducks behind

the lilacs, hides
until her nose tickles. She giggles. "I'm not here."

She runs away,
her brother behind her, bigger, stronger, older,

arms out, ready to catch
her, ready to grab the end of her shirt, anything

of her. They fall,
arms and legs, legs and arms. Laughter.

Grass stains
on her knees, his elbow. I watch. Remember the first day

she was here,
her skin dark like his, their eyes almond-shaped.

She wouldn't look
at my white face or her dad's, but reached

for her brother,
let him hug her, rest his cheek on her head,

put her cheek on his chest.
No need for words in any language. They understood.

They play.
He cries. Pretends. She squats, rubs his hair. "You okay?"

"Fooled you!"
He runs away. Her eyes narrow in fake anger,

her fists clench. She is ready.
"Come and catch me." She runs after him.

They fall, laugh,
their bodies tangled in joy.

Estrangement Letter

Dear Mom,

This letter is stained with orange
marmalade, coffee creamer.

The letters drop into blots,
lie crumpled in the trash.

This letter may be burned
later, the fire dangerous, close.

This letter is the echo
of your whimper, weakness.

This letter has the shape
of your back in it, the rounded

slump of your shadow, the sound
of you forgetting me.

This letter tastes like rage.
This letter is nothing.

Bedtime

"Mom, do you know that only three percent
of the water on the earth is safe
to drink, only three? We could die. We could die
without that water, without what we need. Did you know
Mina is going to dance in the talent show, that Abraham
is going to play the ukulele? My teacher
got a new kitten. It's black with white
paws. It's cute. She showed us a picture. Tomorrow
we have a math test. Mom?"
      "Mmmm."
"Mom, Olivia got new shoes. They are pink.
With glitter. I want some. Can I have some? Today
for lunch was pizza. I ate two pieces. On Friday
if we're all good, we get an extra recess. Mom,
do you know something? A man of war is a fish,
not a man. Isn't that funny? Mom, mom,
mom? Can we make chocolate chip cookies
tomorrow? We haven't done that
in a long time. I am craving them!"
      "Just one more thing. Then we have to be quiet."
"Okay let me think. I'm thinking.
Mom? Can you stay
in my room until
I go to sleep?"
      "I'm right here."

Enough

"That's enough now. Stop. No more,
young lady. You should know better."
Please? I begged, my lip quivering. I was pretty
enough; people said I looked like you,
but not too pretty, of course.
You kept a record of your rights,
my wrongs. Your blessings, evidence
of goodness, worn proudly to church
like patent leather shoes, perfectly
shined. I was hungry, wanted
a hug, a story, a happy ending,
enough. "Too much," you said, wiped a spot
of lipstick from above your lip, smoothed
your rouge. The sparrows
would have never asked
for more. Why couldn't I be content
with what you decided I was worth? Wanting
was vanity, selfish ambition, pride
certain to lead to disgrace. Your guilt
was your perfume, your jewelry wishes
I could never grant. You left me
with a love like candy, said if I wanted
it enough I'd know the right way to hold
it, that it would fill me. Your love was heaviest
when there was nothing left.

Fall

In the early days of September, I glow
like the leaves' rust and yellow and bright red.
I know it won't be long until it snows.
That crabapple goo looks like you bled

on the oak floor. Was it the new sneakers,
flip flops, the heels my daughter needed
to turn eight? Go play now. I'll be in the bleachers
watching the seasons change, the sky bright blue,

yet cool. She climbs, falls, tries again, awaits
another scrape, the pink scooter, the bike
always, always, ridden with heels, eight not eight
without them. By the fence is the old trike

rusted, red paint faded, a stool. She leaps.
"Mom! Did you see me?" In her grin, time creeps.

Welcome to Puberty

Welcome to the pimple on your chin,
two hairs in your armpit, a beginning,
an end of the childhood you knew. Welcome
to the rage that takes you
from the hugs I'll still give
if you choose, when you want
them, when no one is watching, when your body
allows affection. Welcome
to puberty, my little boy, not
so little anymore. Just yesterday, while we read
about the *Titanic*, the iceberg, the sinking,
that horrible, agonizing sinking, you cried,
leaned your increasing weight against me, scrunched
down to lay your cheek on my shoulder. I stopped
reading to feel the tickle of your hair
in my ear. I want to keep that moment,
what we've both already lost, hold
you on pause. Welcome to inconsolable sadness,
over a cancelled playdate, a girl who smiled
at another boy. Stomp to your room. "You
don't understand!" Creep back to me, a book
in your hand. "Read to me?"

To Fly
A ghazal

Like Icarus near the clouds, I dream of flying,
playing with the hawks, a mouse below screaming and flying.

My body weightless, joints flexible, face smooth, hands strong
on childhood's ceiling, my hope's jet stream, flying

high even higher. I dance on blue mist.
I won't fall. Dream's beauty smiles at my screams, flying

turns them into laughter, trust. Daughter, your small hand
wraps my dreams in your potential, flying

like a gull, a sparrow, common, overlooked. Neither
of us will forget how to get home again. Flying,

we will not let it grow too late. You let go to land. It is nearly
time for you to dream your own adventures, to fly.

Shawna Ervin writes both nonfiction and poetry. She is an MFA candidate in the Rainier Writers Workshop low-residency program, a Pushcart nominee, and received a fellowship from the Sustainable Arts Foundation to attend the Mineral School residency. Her work has appeared in *Tampa Review, Talking River, Evening Street Review, Hiram Poetry Review, Front Porch, The Delmarva Review, Summerset Review,* and *Superstition Review.* She lives in Denver with her family.

CPSIA information can be obtained
at www.ICGtesting.com
Printed in the USA
JSHW011920090120
3442JS00005B/49